Author: Eliud A. Montoya

THE 16 FUNDAMENTAL DOCTRINES EXPLAINED

WORKBOOK

Student's name:

_____

Palabra Pura
palabra-pura.com
2020

The 16 Fundamental Doctrines Explained

Workbook

Copyright © 2020 by Eliud A. Montoya.

All rights reserved.

International Rights Reserved.

ISBN: 978-1-951372-15-6

Scripture quotations from the KING JAMES VERSION, public domain.

No part of this book may be reproduced by any means, including but not limited to mechanical or electronic, including storage information and systems or reproduction, without prior authorization from the author.

The content of this workbook is based on the book *The 16 fundamental doctrines explained*. Copyright © 2017 by Eliud A. Montoya.

Graphic design: Iuliana Sagaidak
Editorial House: Palabra Pura, https://www.palabra-pura.com/

CATEGORY: RELIGION / Christian Theology / Systematic.

PRINTED IN THE UNITED STATES OF AMERICA

Preface

1. Currently, Pentecostal groups collectively represent a very large percentage of total evangelical Christianity worldwide.
   ☐ True ☐ False

The Old Paths

2. When the Church began?_____.

The Resting Periods on the Path

3. The Pentecostal doctrine was configured in the _____ of the _____ century.
4. To believe and live the doctrine is _____ and _____ for unbelievers.
5. John 15:19 says: "_____".

The Doctrine is a Path of Victory

6. Those who fail, their objective is to _____ _____, and even attempt to establish their failure as a _____. Yet failure does not belong in the path of the true _____ of God because it is not about our abilities, it is about a simple and full _____ in the merits of Christ and of the benefits of His _____ and _____.

The Glories of the Doctrine

7. The doctrine does not allow mixtures and will always remain _____ to actions, thoughts, _____ or elucidation by man.
8. The doctrine contradict science.
   ☐ True ☐ False
9. How does the doctrine approach to scientific development?_____.

I The Inspiration of the Scripture

1. The Scriptures—the Old Testament like the New Testament—are our norm of _____ and _____.

2. 2 Timothy 3:16-17 says: "All scripture is given by inspiration of _____, and is profitable for _____, for reproof, for correction, for instruction in _____: That the man of God may be perfect, thoroughly furnished unto _____ _____."

I. A.

3. John 14:6 "Jesus saith unto him, _____."

4. Why should we search the Scriptures? (John 5:39) _____.

5. The center of the Scriptures is _____.

6. Write down some of the figures of Christ revealed in the following books of the Old Testament:
   Genesis: _____;
   Exodus: _____;
   Joshua: _____ _____;
   1st and 2nd Samuel: _____;
   Psalms _____;
   Song of Solomon: _____ _____;
   Isaiah: _____;
   Daniel: _____ _____;
   Joel: _____;
   Jonah: _____;
   Malachi: _____.

I. B.

7. Who did give us understanding of the Father? _____.

8. Who was the first man to make a covenant with God? _____.

9. David's actions are doctrine for us.
   ☐ True   ☐ False

10. Much of our doctrine, contained in the New Testament, is based in the _____ _____.

11. We take _____ from the Old Testament regarding the actions of pious men, taking as _____ their errors.

12. We must always have present that the Old

Testament should be read to be understood _____ _____ _____, always taking into account the benefits of the _____, the _____ and the advent of the _____ .

I. C.

13. Through the Scriptures we become familiar with the _____ and _____ of God.

14. Match (with a line) the characteristics of God's nature to the corresponding Bible verse:

    Almighty — Ps. 139:7-12
    All knowing — Gen. 21:33
    Omnipresent — Rev. 19:6
    Alpha y Omega — Rev. 1:8
    Eternal — Ps. 27:4
    Without beginning
    or end of days — Rom. 11:33
    Invisible — 1 Tim. 6:16
    A Spirit-based Being — Heb. 7:3
    Immutable — Isa. 55:9
    Beautiful — John 4:24
    Incomprehensible — Mal. 3:6-7

15. What characteristics of God's character can be found in these verses?
    Titus 1:2 - absolutely truthful *(example)*;
    Neh. 9:30-31 _____;
    1 Thes. 5:23 _____;
    1 John 4:8 _____;
    Ps. 22:3 _____;
    Ps. 107:1 _____;
    Ex. 34:14 _____;
    Rom. 11:34 _____;
    Rom. 16:27 _____;
    Rom. 12:19 _____;
    Rom. 1:18 _____;
    Gen. 18:25 _____;
    Matt. 7:11 _____.

I. D.

16. His decrees are firm and He will never overstep them.
    ☐ True   ☐ False

17. Because He is sovereign, He chooses to save some and condemn others.
    ☐ True   ☐ False

18. We should be able to understand that His sovereignty _____ when He, through His own will _____ His decrees.

19. We must be careful in placing all things _____ and to do so we must use the _____ with skill.

I. E.

20. What was most important out of the Law of Moses? (Matt. 23:23) _____, _____, and _____.

21. Summarize all of the Law of Moses into two commandments: _____ _____ _____.

22. Write down a list of sins based on following verses: Gal. 5:19-21; 1 Cor. 6:9-10; 2 Cor. 12:20; 1 Tim. 1:9-10; 1 Tim. 6:4; Titus 3:3; 1 Pet. 2:1; Rev. 21:8; and Rev. 22:15 _____ _____ _____ _____

_____
_____
_____
_____
_____
_____
_____
_____
_____
_____
_____
_____
_____
_____.

23. There are things which are not inherently sinful, but which distance us from God.
    ☐ True ☐ False

24. 1 Corinthians 10:23 says: "All things are _____ for me, but all things are not _____: all things are _____, _____ for me, but all things _____ not".

25. They are things that are used by Satan as _____ to tempt us or place us in a situation _____ _____.

26. If we do not do what Mark 16:15 tells us, this is also a sin (disobedience).
    ☐ True ☐ False

I. F.

27. The Scriptures serve as a _____ that guides us to the will of God.

28. Romans 10:17 says: "_____
_____
_____
_____."

29. Reading, memorizing, reciting, scrutinizing, studying and listening to Scripture helps _____.

30. What is needed to please God? _____.

31. Who do we become (according to Revelation 5:10)? _____.

32. What, according to Deuteronomy 17:18-19, do we have to do every day? _____
_____
_____.

33. Match the characteristics of the Scriptures to the Biblical verses in which they are mentioned:

    a lamp   Deut. 8:3
    fire   Eph. 6:17
    a hammer   Prov. 6:23b
    a seed   1 Pet. 2:2
    a sword   Jer. 5:14
    bread   Ps. 119:105
    milk   Jer. 23:29b
    light   Luke 8:11

I. G.

34. Every Christian should dedicate time _____ _____ to scrutinize the _____.

35. Salvation is through _____ and the Scriptures mark the _____.

36. Mention some key verses in order to help someone enter through the door that is Christ: _____
_____

_____
_____.

37. It is not necessary to know Bible verses by memory.
☐ True ☐ False

38. The Holy Spirit always confirms _____ _____ what He wants to make _____ in our minds and hearts.

II The One True God

II. A.

1. Genesis 1:26, "Let us make man in _____ image, after _____ likeness".

2. One of the many names of God, *Elohim*, which is mentioned, more than _____ times in the OT, appears in Hebrew in its _____ form.

II. B.

3. The _____ persons of the trinity are involved in our access to God, in this way Paul says in Ephesians 2:18: "_____ _____ _____ _____".

II. C.

4. Our God is only one God revealed in _____.

5. Romans 3:30a says: "_____ _____,"

II. D.

6. The word "trinity" is a theological term that is not mentioned in the Scriptures and meant to help us quickly identify concepts.
☐ True ☐ False

7. Who resurrected Jesus? _____ _____ _____.

8. The nature of God remains inscrutable and _____ to the human _____.

II. E.

9. There is what can be said to be attributable only to the Father and not the Son nor to the Holy Spirit; that which consists only in the Son and is proper to Him only and not to the Father nor the Holy Spirit; and what is proper to the Holy Spirit and not to the Son nor the Father.
☐ True ☐ False

10. When the trinity is spoken of, _____ _____ between the Father, the Son and the Holy Spirit is what is referred to.

11. Who was eternally the object of the Father's love? _____.

12. The Father, the Son and the Holy Spirit are intricately _____, they are three persons yet they are not _____ _____; hey are one God, but _____ in _____ union.

13. Match the lines between Father, Son and the Holy Spirit with the biblical verses in which

they are mentioned:

The Son was engendered by the Father	John 5:18
The Father loves the Son	Ps. 2:7
The Son belongs to His very essential nature	John 5:30
The Son cooperates with the Father	John 5:20
The Son is under His authority	John 16:13
All creation worships the Father just as it worships the Son	John 8:18
The Holy Spirit takes what he hears from the Father and the Son	John 16:14
The Holy Spirit glorifies the Son	John 5:23

II. F.

14. When we refer to the title "Lord Jesus Christ", we refer to the Father, the Son and the Holy Spirit.
☐ True ☐ False

15. Acts 16:31 says: "And they said: _____ ".

16. Christ had, before being incarnated, only the _____ nature. However, he also acquired _____ nature.

17. In Luke 1:32 Christ is identified as "Son of _____", and in Matthew 9:6 as "_____".

18. He is therefore _____% God and _____% man.

19. The book of Hebrews speaks just as much to the divine character of Jesus Christ as it does of His humanity.
☐ True ☐ False

20. Write down the words "divine character" or "humanity" based on the content of the following verses:
Heb. 5:7 _____;
Heb. 7:3 _____.

II. G.

21. Jesus is really God made flesh.
☐ True ☐ False

22. To deny the relationship between the Father and the Son, is to deny _____ of the Being of God, which is equivalent to not _____.

II. H.

23. Put the sentences in order:
____ Jesus sent the Holy Spirit
____ Jesus have purged us with His blood
____ Jesus was buried and resurrected
____ Jesus took His seat at the right hand of God

24. Every time we bend our knees before _____ we are giving glory to God the _____, since He _____ Christ.

25. 1 Peter 3:22 says: "Who is gone into heaven, and is on the right hand of God; _____ and _____ and _____ being made subject unto him".

26. Acts 2:36b: "that God hath made the same Jesus, whom ye have crucified, _____ _____".

II. I.

27. The Son of God appeared to destroy the works of the _____ (1 John 3:8) and to recover the glory that Satan _____ _____.

28. The eternal plan of God is fulfilled in Christ Jesus, when He performs our _____ _____ (Rom. 5:10).

29. God's plan has come to an end.
☐ True ☐ False

30. Put the sentences in order:
____ death will be destroyed;
____ Christ still must reign on earth for a thousand years;
____ the Son himself will be subject to the Father;
____ all His enemies will be put under His feet.

31. Who glorifies whom in the following passages?

Acts 3:13: the _____ glorifies the _____;
John 16:14-15: the _____ glorifies the _____;
John 17:4: the _____ glorifies the _____.

II. J.

32. All of the titles and names of God are attributed to Christ, for which He receives the same honor as the Father.
☐ True ☐ False

33. John 5:22-23: "For the Father judgeth no man, but hath committed all judgment unto the _____: That all men should _____ the Son, even as they _____ the Father. He that _____ the Sun, _____ the Father which hath sent him."

III. The Deity of the Lord Jesus Christ

1. The Scriptures teach us that Jesus Christ is _____. The existing eternal God, creator and sustainer of _____. He is one with the _____ and the _____ _____, and in their eternal communion.

2. Put the letters in the correct column:

As God, Jesus Christ is:	As a man, Jesus Christ is:

A) The first-born Son of Mary; B) The first-born of the new spiritual creation of God; C) the only begotten Son of the Father; D) The firstborn in the reconciliation of all things; E) who was sent to the world to save us from our sins.

III. A.

3. Through whom did God prophesy that the sign about Messiah would be that He would be born of a virgin? _____.

4. The virgin Mary was the chosen _____ _____ by God.

III. B.

5. Christ never had the opportunity to sin.
   ☐ True ☐ False

6. 1 Peter 2:22 says: "Who did no _____, neither was _____ found in his _____;"

7. The sinless life of Christ makes Him the _____ who takes away the _____ of the world (John 1:29).

III. C.

8. We do not see anyone else in history doing as many miracles as He did.
   ☐ True ☐ False

9. Acts 3:15 "And killed the _____ _____, whom God hath _____ _____ whereof we are witnesses".

10. The most evident proof of His divinity was His _____ (Acts 2:24).

III. D.

11. God made Jesus sin so that we would be made _____.

12. Romans 5:8 says: "_____ _____ _____ _____ _____ _____".

13. A man can not save another man and none

is worthy to put our trust in him for our eternal destiny, except in Him, who is not only Man but God.

☐ True ☐ False

III. E.

14. Jesus's death is figurative, a symbolism.

    ☐ True ☐ False

15. The Son of God can never die, and cannot cease to be God even for a moment, but _____ _____ died.

16. John 19:32-33 Why didn't the soldiers break Jesus' legs? _____ _____.

17. Link events to the corresponding Scripture:

    | His dead body was removed from the cross | 1 Cor. 15:4 |
    | He was wrapped in a clean sheet | Matt. 27:60 |
    | He was burried | 1 Cor. 15:5-8 |
    | He rose on the third day | Matt. 27:50 |
    | He appeared alive to many for 40 days | Matt. 27:59 |

18. What was the sign given by Christ in Matt. 12:38-40? _____.

III. F.

19. "And no man hath _____ up to heaven, but he that _____ from heaven, even the Son of man which _____ in heaven" (John 3:13).

20. The Son of God never ceased to be in heaven.

    ☐ True ☐ False

21. Hebrews 1:3 is a powerful passage proving the _____ of Christ.

III. G.

22. There are at least **seven** passages of the Bible where the divinity of Christ is declared with absolute clarity. Write them down. _____ _____ _____ _____ _____.

III. H.

23. Who can we worship? _____.

24. When Paul and Barnabas were in Lystra, they agreed to be worshiped by the crowd (Acts 14:11).

    ☐ True ☐ False

25. Jesus Christ received adoration, which is offered only to God himself.

    ☐ True ☐ False

26. Matt. 14:33: "Then they that were in the ship came and worshipped him, saying, _____ _____".

27. Thomas called Jesus "God".

    ☐ True ☐ False

III. I.

28. God not only _____ goodness or kindness but He and He alone _____ good.

29. Christ does not deny that He is _____ and that He has the same _____ of God but makes the rich reflect on His _____ in this passage.

IV The Fall of Man

1. According to Genesis 1:26; 2:7, how was man created? _____ _____ _____.

2. Man was created perfect.
   ☐ True ☐ False

IV. A.

3. Man by nature is bad and it was always so.
   ☐ True ☐ False

4. God created a man and woman _____ _____ (Gen. 1:31).

5. Link with a line the comforts of the human being before the fall with the corresponding Scripture:

   Gen. 1:29   a place to live
   Gen. 2:8   the commandments
   Gen. 2:15, 19   food
   Gen. 2:18, 21, 22   work
   Gen. 1:28; 2:17   human company

IV. B.

6. The image that man has was inspired by _____ (Col. 1:15).

7. Romans 6:13: "Neither yield ye your members as instruments of unrighteousness _____: but yield yourselves unto _____, as those that are alive from the dead, and your members as instruments of _____."

8. The human being is constituted, in addition to the physical body, of a _____ and a _____.

9. The soul: is the center of _____, of _____ and of the _____.

10. Our intellect is the _____, _____ and _____ center.

11. Will or rather, free will is the human capacity that allows us to _____ _____.

12. In the son or daughter of God, the spirit (the other part of man) intervenes powerfully in _____, which is _____ _____ and this differentiates him from those who do not know God.

13. The spirit is the part of the human being that may or may not be connected with God.
    ☐ True ☐ False

14. When the human being is not in Christ, his spirit is _____.

15. Romans 8:10: "And if Christ be in you, the

body is dead because of _____, but the Spirit is life because of _____."

IV. C.

16. The goal that God gave Man was to fill the earth and subdue it. Dominate over creation.
☐ True ☐ False

17. Genesis 1:28: "And God blessed them, and God said unto them, _____: and have dominion over the fish of the sea, and over the fowl of the air, and over every living thing that moveth upon the earth."

18. Knowledge of good and evil was necessary to have wisdom.
☐ True ☐ False

IV. D.

19. Satan was originally full of light and splendor, a cherub, one of the most beautiful angels created by God.
☐ True ☐ False

20. Satan believe that he could be like _____. He was deceived by his very _____ that suggested he could put his _____ next to God's, that he could be like _____ _____ himself.

21. Which idea Satan transmitted to Eva, and she to her husband? _____.

22. The sin is born of an insane _____ of a deception.

23. The devil operates, making the _____ believe that sin gives more _____ than staying in the _____ of God.

IV. E.

24. Man was created to have _____ with God (Gen. 3:8).

25. Proverbs 16:4a says: "The Lord hath made all things for _____".

26. God wanted Man to understand that the greatest satisfaction was in _____.

27. God abandoned Adam and Eve in the garden, providing enough for them to survive and then move away.
☐ True ☐ False

IV. F.

28. Man was deceived, so he **can** justify his sin.
☐ True ☐ False

29. After sin, the nature of man is turned into a _____, of _____ and _____.

30. Jeremiah 17:9 says: "The _____ is deceitful above all things and _____: who can know it?"

31. Romans 5:12 says, "Wherefore, as by _____ _____ sin entered into the world, and _____ by sin; and so _____ passed upon _____, for that all have sinned".

32. The way of living in sin is an inevitable inheritance of our parents, and this sin carries with it death.
☐ True ☐ False

IV. G.

33. Physical consequences of sin: mankind will be subjected to _____ (Rev. 2:22) and to _____ (Gen. 3:19).

34. Consequences in the **environment**: The animals became _____ who would attack _____; The earth was _____ because of sin (Gen. 3:17).

35. Consequences in the **government**: The woman would be _____ to the husband.

36. Consequences of sin (**physical and psychological enjoyment**):
    a) for woman: the physical and psychological enjoyment of procreation and giving birth would become an _____ _____.
    b) for men: the physical and psychological enjoyment of work would be reduced to a _____ _____.

37. Consequences of sin (**Moral**): the human being would have a tendency to _____ _____.

38. Consequences of sin (**Spiritual**): man is _____ by nature (Luke 9:60; Col. 2:13).

39. Every person is born a saint, but when he sins for the first time, he becomes a sinner. ☐ True ☐ False

IV. H.

40. In Christ Jesus our relationship to God is _____ (Col. 1:20).

41. God revealed the redemption plan for humanity:
    • There would be a cosmic enmity between the seed of the woman, (_____) and that of the serpent (_____ _____).

    • God speaks of two violent acts:
    1) with the _____, who would be wounded in the _____;
    2) and with the seed of the woman, _____, who would be wounded in the _____.

V. The Salvation of Man

1. Pure and well intentioned efforts will bring us closer to God.
   ☐ True ☐ False

2. Ephesians 2:12 says man without Christ is _____ _____ _____ _____ _____.

3. A person becomes sinner not precisely because he sins, but because _____ _____.

4. Being a sinner is part of the Adamic nature, so Christ could not be a descendant of Adam, because He had to be sinless.
   ☐ True ☐ False

5. How do we know we are sinning? _____ _____ _____ (Rom. 2:15).

6. Man will sin since he has the use of _____ because that is _____ _____, and will commit sin immediately upon _____ _____.

7. In order to interrupt that road to hell, we have to _____ along _____, _____ and let God through Christ _____ _____.

8. Romans 5:19 says: "For as by one _____ many were made _____, so by the _____ _____, shall many be _____ _____".

V. A.

9. John 14:6 says: "_____ _____ _____ _____ _____".

10. The Scriptures guide us along_____ _____, which is Christ himself.

11. Salvation opens the door to:
    a)_____
    (John 3:15-16);
    b) _____
    _____ (Rom. 5:10);
    c) _____
    (Matt. 18:23-35);
    d) _____
    _____ (Rev. 20:15);

e) _____ (Rom. 5:8);

f) _____ (Rom. 8:39);

g) _____ (Rom. 5:1);

h) _____ (Col. 1:14);

i) _____ (1 Cor. 1:2);

j) _____ (John 3:7).

12. Without Christ all were made enemies of God (Is. 34:2).
    ☐ True ☐ False

13. No name was inscribed in the book of life until _____ decided to _____ in Jesus Christ as _____, because only through Him do we have salvation.

14. The Book of Life always has existed.
    ☐ True ☐ False

15. To be saved means_____ and for those who _____ there is no condemnation. The body is _____ because of sin, but the spirit lives because of righteousness. They are already _____, they are blessed with every spiritual blessing.

16. Every person without salvation is classified by God as _____ (1 Cor. 6:9), _____ (Rom. 5:6) and _____ (1 Pet. 4:18).

17. The Bible tells us that there is none who are righteous. What does this mean? _____ _____ _____.

18. Man was sold under _____ (Rom. 7:14).

19. Paul speaks of his _____ _____ in Romans 7.

20. Jesus bought us with _____ _____ (Eph. 1:7).

21. A person who is saved _____ _____ (Rom. 6:14) and has _____ over it and has been _____ by Christ (1 Cor. 6:9-11).

22. The Word tells us that our sanctification is accomplished:
    ♦ By _____ of Christ (1 John. 1:7);
    ♦ By the _____ (2 Thes. 2:13).

23. We are all sinners.
    ☐ True ☐ False

24. To be saved means to live _____ _____ over sin through the precious blood of Christ and through the power of the Spirit of God in us.

25. Sanctification is not by our works but _____.

26. When Christ died on the cross He potentially saved the _____, taking the place of _____; However, only those who repent and believe in Him are _____.

V. B.

27. Where in the Old Testament doest it says: "the just shall live by his faith"? _____.

28. How was Abraham saved? _____.

29. In Hebrews 11:24-26 we can see that Moses believed in Christ before His coming.
☐ True ☐ False

30. The men and women of the Old Testament never fully enjoyed the benefits of Calvary, and although they reached some promises (Heb. 11:33), they did not receive all the promises that God gives through Christ (Rom. 15:8; Gal. 3:16; Col. 1:20; Heb. 6:12) to the church.
☐ True ☐ False

31. What was the purpose of the law? _____.

32. Who was able to keep completely the Law of Moses? _____.

V. C.
33. Acts 4:12 says "_____".

V. D.
34. Acts 17:30b: "... now commandeth _____".

35. 2 Corinthians 5:14 means there is now opportunity to all men.
☐ True ☐ False

36. God, since before the foundation of the world, determined that _____ would be saved and that it is our _____ that ultimately determines whether this salvation is effective or not in us. In other words, predestination is for _____, but only those _____ and _____ in Jesus Christ are saved.

V. E.
37. How many conditions are indispensable for the miracle of salvation to take place? _____.

38. What conditions are indispensable for the miracle of salvation to take place? _____ _____ and _____.

39. The human being is composed of _____.

40. The spirit without Christ is _____ and the soul is _____ by an erroneous conception of _____ and of God.

41. The excuses a man could give to sin are valid before God: He understands and acept them.
☐ True ☐ False

<u>Repentance:</u>

42. *Thoughts:*
a) The gospel manages to penetrate the mind of the sinner who comes to the conclusion that he is _____;
b) The penitent sinner begins to see God as a _____ who rightly condemns him for _____ (Ps. 7:11).
c) The penitent sinner now sees sin as something _____, _____, and _____;
d) The repentant sinner genuinely sees himself as one who _____

_____. Now he understands that he is in danger of becoming a prisoner of hell and wants at all costs _____ _____;

e) He thinks that he must_____ to God with all his heart, because that will be _____ for his situation (Luke 15:17).

43. *Emotions:*
   a) The penitent sinner feels a deep_____ _____ (2 Cor. 7:10);
   b) He _____ himself before the Almighty;
   c) The repentant sinner begins to feel _____ for his own sins.

44. *Human-Will:*
   1) The penitent sinner _____ _____ sin.
   2) By hearing and believing the Word he supports his repentance with _____.

45. Christ commands that our preaching be of _____ and _____ of sins (Luke 24:47).

46. The preaching of the gospel includes the explanation of the seriousness of the human condition. Not only for the sins that the sinner has done, but for his own sinful condition by his Adamic nature.
   ☐ True ☐ False

Faith:

47. Faith is a state of total _____ in the _____ (Heb. 11:1); is born of _____ (Rom. 10:17); and being fully _____ that God is _____ to do all that He _____ (Rom. 4:21).

48. The repentant sinner seizes salvation without _____ of any _____, only by _____ in Christ; by faith he _____ the sacrifice that Christ made _____;

49. Christ at that moment becomes his only and sufficient _____; and a _____ _____ joy floods his being. It is the _____ _____ entering his life for the first time.

50. God makes him a _____ ; his spirit is _____ and his natural _____ with God has begun.

51. The only action you need to take is to get on your knees before the Son of God, confess him as Lord and Savior and totally surrender your life to Him.
   ☐ True ☐ False

V. F.

52. There is no spurious salvation. It is always genuine.
   ☐ True ☐ False

53. 2 Corinthians 7:10: "For godly sorrow worketh _____ not to be repented of; but the sorrow of the world worketh _____".

54. *False Repentance:*
   a) He feels like a _____;
   b) He still _____ sin;
   c) He is not willing to ask for _____ _____, nor to _____ _____ his sins, or restitute the

wrong done to their neighbor;

d) He feels remorse for his actions, but ___ _____;

e) He stops sinning not because he _____ the sin, but because he fears the _____ that it produces.

f) He only leaves some practices that seemed the worst, but still _____ _____;

g) He leaves sin for one day but the next one _____, Then, on Sunday, he goes to the meeting and asks _____ _____ but returns to the same cycle time and time again;

h) He feels the Christian life and the commandments of the Lord are a _____ _____ instead of a _____ _____.

i) He still has a hardened _____. Maybe he has _____, but not a broken and _____ heart before the Lord.

55. *Spurious faith:*

a) He does not totally place his trust in Christ for salvation, but sees Him as _____ _____.

b) He fails to understand that only by _____ in Him it is possible to be saved. He is helped by other things that he considers as _____ _____.

c) He has an _____ faith. Faith transforms us and not only convinces us.

d) His faith does not produce _____.

When a person has a genuine faith it gives him joy.

V. G.
Salvation Evidence:

56. He who is born again obeys by nature _____ of the Lord and abides in God, and the Spirit that has been given testifies within him about _____.

57. Before he subjected all things to _____ _____. Now he accepts the truth of God without questioning.

58. The _____ of God is poured into his heart (Rom. 5:5). His spirit has _____ and needs to worship God.

59. The child of God _____, not moved by _____ or by a social cause, but because of the _____ _____ he now has in Christ Jesus.

60. The new son or daughter of God has a _____ like Christ's, a teachable heart, a heart that is willing to _____ the Lord in everything.

External Evidence of Salvation

61. _____ is a public act that manifests the authentic feeling of a repentant heart that has believed in Jesus Christ as his personal Savior.

62. Our faith in Christ could be something private, kept in the heart, what we do not want anyone to know about.

☐ True   ☐ False

63. Salvation could be aborted when someone, subjected to the test of confession, fails because of fear.
☐ True ☐ False

64. God wants the sinner to _____ his guilt before Him and his _____ in Jesus Christ as his only means of salvation.

65. Salvation requires _____ and _____ in Christ Jesus, however, _____ _____ is the demonstration of that faith.

66. 2 Corinthians 4:13 says: "We having the same spirit of faith, according as it is written, I believed, and _____ _____; we also believe, and therefore _____,".

67. Those who refuse to confess Christ publicly as their personal Savior, what are they demonstrating? _____.

68. Confession is just about the "sinner's prayer".
☐ True ☐ False

69. The confession is mainly done within _____ _____.

70. Luke 9:26: "_____ _____ _____ _____ _____ _____ _____".

71. Confession is _____.

72. Match the verse with its location in the Bible

"For by thy words thou shalt be justified, and by thy words thou shalt be condemned" Matt. 12:34

"Death and life are in the power of the tongue" Matt. 12:37

"For our of the abundance of the heart the mouth speaketh" Prov. 18:21

73. We have the power of God to live a holy life.
☐ True ☐ False

74. Although he was saved by faith, he is _____ _____ and deals with them.

V. H.

75. Every Christian understands that his salvation is _____ in Jesus Christ. As long as he or she _____ in Christ and remains _____ to the true vine that is the Lord, salvation will be secured in Him.

76. John 10:28 says: "And I give unto them eternal life; and they shall never perish, neither _____ _____".

77. Eternal life began from the moment _____ _____.

78. Jude 1:24 says "Now unto him that is able to _____, and present you _____ before the presence of his glory with exceeding joy".

79. God assures us that his power will _____ _____ until we reach salvation.

80. Based on Romans 8:35-39, Who shall separate us from the love of Christ? _____.

81. While we are in the Lord, the battle is won ahead of time.
☐ True ☐ False

V. I.

82. "... but he that _____ _____, shall be saved" (Matt. 10:22b).

83. The Christian life has a cost of _____ that not everyone is willing to pay.

85. Christ tells us that the only way to bear fruit is _____.

86. Faith produces fruit and fruit is a demostration of _____ and our _____ _____ in Him.

87. The requierement to finally reach the salavtion is to _____ _____ _____.

88. In 1 Corintios 15:3-8 Paul reminds everyone what the Gospel consists of: the _____ _____ _____ _____.

89. The Gospel of Christ cannot be perverted .
☐ True ☐ False

90. "Whosoever transgresseth, and abideth not in the doctrine of Christ, _____ He that abideth in the doctrine of Christ, he hath _____ _____" (2 John 1:9).

V. J.

91. There is a possitility that we will return to the same state where we were before we were saved if _____ _____.

92. Salvation cannot be lost.
☐ True ☐ False

93. Can the will of someone separate us from the love of God? _____ _____.

94. When a person is outside of Christ, he has given his will to _____ _____ and _____ (Eph. 2:1-3; 2 Ti. 2:26), but in Christ, he becomes a servant of _____ (Rom. 6:15-18).

95. Every day we make decisions and these can be of _____: to go to Christ or _____ to separate ourselves from Him until we stop _____.

96. We can maintain a holy life through the power of the _____.

97. The flesh is extirpated when we come to Christ.
☐ True ☐ False

98. _____ continue to be in us, but through our faith in Christ _____ and do not allow them to force us to sin.

99. It takes a _____ to slip, it is not _____.

100. Salvation can be neglected.
☐ True ☐ False

101. In 1 Ti. 4:1 the Bible tells us about _____ _____.

102. Is there any unpardonable sin (Matt. 12:31)? _____

_____.

103. The blasphemy against the Holy Spirit is to _____
_____.

104. It is a _____ terrain to speak ill of the _____ and of the miracles that occur in their ministries.

105. A sign that someone blasphemed against the Holy Spirit is that he or she does not ___ _____ of any sin.

106. Who leads us to repentance (John 16:7-8)? _____.

107. Words that do not promote the faith but destroy it, they are the cause of a curse instead of a blessing.
☐ True ☐ False

108. Can one who has believed in Christ say words that destroy faith? _____
_____
_____
_____.

109. If the Holy Spirit is saddened or grieved, there is no _____ and there is _____.

110. If there is no fruit, then _____ _____ (John 15:6).

111. The salvation of someone who now walks in the Lord can be lost because of the clumsiness of other Christians, because they do not walk according to love.
☐ True ☐ False

112. "... the Lord having saved the people out of the land of Egypt, afterward destroyed them that _____" (Jude 1:5b).

113. Jude describes people who do not admit to be _____, but who feed themselves; those who do not admit the _____ _____ of the servants of God; those who do not bear fruit and who have experienced _____ twice (Jude 1:12).

114. 2 Peter 2:20 says: "For if after they have _____ the pollutions of the world through the knowledge of the Lord and Saviour Jesus Christ, they are _____ _____ and overcome, the latter end is _____ with them than the beginning".

115. People who were true children of God, who lived in holiness and walked in truth could be astray and start to teach false doctrine.
☐ True ☐ False

116. Evidently one who is _____ is the one who first sailed well, while the Captain of his ship was Christ.

117. There are evil servants of God.
☐ True ☐ False

118. Draw a line to join the biblical verses with the corresponding topic.

A) They departed from the faith — Eph. 4:29-30
B) They have blasphamed against the Holy Spirit — Jude 1:5-6
C) The Holy Spirit is grieved — 2 Pet. 2:20-22
D) Stumbling stones — 1 Ti. 4:1
E) Unbelievers — Rom. 14:15
F) They go back to sin — Heb. 6:4-6

G) They teach false doctrine — 1 Tim. 1:18-19
H) Those who are shipwrecked — Matt. 24:48
I) Evil servants — 2 Tim. 2:17-18

119. A person who has lost his salvation can no longer be restored.
☐ True ☐ False

V. K.

120. The loss of salvation is a process.
☐ True ☐ False

121. Occasional sins are signs of _____.

122. The carnal Christian lives in constant _____, because if he dies or the Lord comes and finds him in sin, _____ _____ with Christ (Luke 12:37).

123. If the Christian does not confess his sin _____ from it then he will continue to disintegrate and his heart _____ more and more.

124. The Christian knows that he is _____ _____, because his heart does not rebuke him, that is the Holy Spirit gives _____ (1 John 3:20).

V. L.

125. The Bible teaches us some signs that tell us that we are going the wrong way and we have to return to the right path immediately. Which are they?
A. _____
_____;
B. _____
_____;
C. _____
_____;
D. _____
_____;
E. _____
_____;
F. _____
_____;
G. _____
_____.

126. Which is our spiritual food? _____.

127. If we do not feed ourselves spiritually we can not _____ to Christ.

128. It is essential for new believers to be fed with the Word of God daily, but not so much for those who know many verses by memory.
☐ True ☐ False

129. _____ have been the stumbling block for many to become only hearers of the Word and not doers.

130. What Bible verse says: "But they that will be rich fall into temptation and a snare, and into many foolish and hurtful lusts, which drown men in destruction and perdition" _____.

131. The Lord Jesus reminds us that the only way to be spiritually strong is to use the instrument of _____.

132. _____, says the Lord, will keep us from temptation. That is, sin will not be _____ for us to

make us fall into it.

133. God commands us to bond with _____ _____ and strengthen each other.

134. The things of this world can be attractive.
☐ True ☐ False

135. Being ashamed of the gospel and of Christ is a very serious fault and a sign that _____ _____ _____.

VI. The Ordinances of the Church

1. Unlike other creeds, in which external rites and practices take on great importance for the salvation of the individual, we believe that any external practice will never be something included as a requisite for one's own salvation or that of any other individual.
   ☐ True ☐ False

2. A sacrament, as understood by other religions, is _____ _____.

3. Ordinance and sacrament are synonyms
   ☐ True ☐ False

4. What is the purpose of the ordinances? _____ _____ _____.

VI. A.

5. What are the three baptisms we can find in the NT?
   - Baptism _____
   - Baptism _____
   - Baptism _____.

6. Who did ordain water baptism for the church? _____.

7. "He that believeth and is baptized shall be saved; but he that believeth not shall be damned". Where is it? _____.

8. Mattew 28:19 says: "_____ _____ _____ _____ _____ _____".

9. Salvation is granted by _____, it is a _____ which is not obtained by _____.

10. Baptism becomes a requirement for salvation when it is a demonstration of our faith.
    ☐ True ☐ False

11. The only reason why a person refuses to be baptized in water is that he or she has not _____.

12. Water baptism is an _____ _____ that symbolizes what has already happened in _____: regeneration by the _____ (Tit. 3:5) and the washing of _____ (Acts 22:16).

13. The baptism in water is a public act of _____ of our faith.

14. Baptism aims to reaffirm:
    ◆ our death to _____ and
    ◆ our new _____.

15. In water baptism we tell _____ we have renounced _____ and decided _____; that this has been posible through the death and resurrection of Jesus and through _____ _____.

16. He who is dead [and remains dead] cannot sin.
☐ True ☐ False

17. Baptism makes us die to the world, sin and the law.
☐ True ☐ False

18. What is the meaning of the moment when we are totally submerged in the water? _____ _____.

19. The Father, the Son and the Holy Spirit are mentioned in each of next Bible verses: Acts 2:38, Acts 10:48, and Acts 19:5.
☐ True ☐ False

20. What verse of the Bible does contain the correct formula of water baptism? _____ _____.

21. What is the correct formula for water baptism? _____ _____ _____.

22. Water baptism must not be total immersion.
☐ True ☐ False

23. What is the meaning of total immersion? _____ _____ _____ _____.

24. Christ has ordained water baptism and everything the Lord has commanded must be obeyed without hesitation.
☐ True ☐ False

25. What does the *Didache* recommend us to do before being baptized? _____ _____
(Didache 7:6).

26. Christ establishes the order of baptism: first the _____ and _____ and after _____.

27. Exist a minimum age to be baptized even if the candidate accomplishes the requirements.
☐ True ☐ False

28. Some churches establish the additional requirement that the newly converted have gained a soul for Christ in order to be a viable candidate for baptism.
☐ True ☐ False

29. The one who has been saved, will never have any objection in baptizing.
☐ True ☐ False

30. What about someone who can be baptized, and is hesitant to do so? _____ _____ _____.

31. When a person should be baptized again?
   A. _____ _____,
   B. _____ _____.

32. If a person has relapsed and then returned to the path, he needs to be baptized again.
☐ True ☐ False

VI. B.

33. The Apostle Paul explains the Holy Supper clearly in _____.

34. Who did established the Holy Supper? _____.

35. What is the purpose of the Holy Supper? _____ _____.

36. Why the Holy Supper is also called the Holy Communion? _____ _____ _____.

37. Why does Paul call it "the cup of blessing"? _____ _____.

38. Every time we take the Holy Communion we are participating in _____ _____ of the Lord.

39. Therefore every time we participate in the Lord's Supper we are remembering that we were saved because _____ _____ shed on the cross and healed by _____ that was broken or wounded by us.

40. The apostle Paul compares the church with _____.

41. Not having communion with our brothers and not showing them love makes us _____ _____ and is proof that we do not walk _____ (1 John 1:8).

42. What distortions of the practice of the Holy Supper were there in Corinth? (1 Cor. 11:17-22)
    - _____ _____;
    - _____ _____;
    - _____ _____.

43. If the Holy Supper is taken disrespectfully and in sin, instead of being _____ _____ for confirmation of our faith in divine healing, will be for _____.

44. 1 Corinthians 11:30 says: "For this cause many are _____ and _____ among you, and _____".

45. Among some Christian denominations, the Holy Supper is given a different meaning. ☐ True   ☐ False

46. What the transubstantiating is about? ____ _____ _____ _____ _____.

47. Christ is received through a ceremony of the Holy Supper. ☐ True   ☐ False

48. Every time we participate in the Holy Communion we have to do it in _____, and thus renew the _____ of the death of Christ in our _____.

VII. The Baptism in the Holy Spirit

1. All Christians have access to the baptism in the Holy Spirit.
   ☐ True   ☐ False

2. God's promise of the Holy Spirit is found in the Old Testament, Where is the Bible verse located? _____ .

3. We should receive the baptism in the Holy Spirit at the exact moment we get saved.
   ☐ True   ☐ False

VII. A.

4. In what Bible verse we found a distinction between baptism in water and baptism in the Holy Spirit? _____ .

5. A person who is saved receives the Holy Spirit in his heart (together with the Father and with the Son, because God is a triune God).
   ☐ True   ☐ False

6. The Scriptures forcefully teach us that the baptism in the Holy Spirit is a _____ _____ and _____ experience.

VII. B.

7. What is required to receive the baptism in the Holy Spirit? _____ .

8. Being baptized in water is a requirement to receive the baptism in the Holy Spirit.
   ☐ True   ☐ False

9. A person cannot be baptized in the Holy Spirit on the same day he received salvation.
   ☐ True   ☐ False

10. A nonconfessed sin will be an _____ to received the baptism in the Holy Spirit (Acts 5:32).

11. It is essential to have a clear conscience to received this baptism.
    ☐ True   ☐ False

12. What does make us overcome sin? (Acts 26:18) _____ .

VII. C.

13. The baptism in the Holy Spirit is simply feeling the presence of God and to have freedom to pray.
    ☐ True   ☐ False

14. Who is the baptizer? (Luke 3:16) _____ .

15. Beside genuine salvation or holiness, what else is needed to receive the baptism in the Holy Spirit? _____ .

VII. D.

16. What are the three elements of a baptism?
    - _____ ,

- _____,
- _____
  _____.

17. In Joel 2:28-29, God speaks of an _____ _____, and in Acts 8:14-16 the experience of baptism in the Holy Spirit is a _____ _____ of the Spirit. In Ephesians 5:18 this experience is the _____, and has to do with _____ _____.

18. In John 7:37-38 the Lord says that being baptized in the Spirit is a _____. What verse in the Old Testament is it referring to? _____.

VII. E.

19. God wants us to be _____ for His baptism and to ask fervently. He wants us to have a _____ to receive His gift.

20. What is the gift that the child of God can get based on Luke 11:13? _____ _____.

21. If we analyze James 1:6-7, how should we ask for the baptism in the Spirit? _____ _____.

22. Faith implies living in the _____ what we are asking for, as if we _____ _____.

VII. F.

23. God tells us in Ephesians 3:16 that He wants us to be "_____ _____ _____".

VII. G.

24. <u>What the baptism in the Spirit is Not for:</u>

   a) _____ _____;
   b) _____ _____;
   c) _____ _____;
   d) _____ _____.

25. What cleanses us from sin? (1 John 1:7) _____.

26. Staying full of the Spirit implies walking in the Spirit and living in holiness.
   ☐ True   ☐ False

27. Feeling good is the purpose of the baptism in the Spirit.
   ☐ True   ☐ False

28. The baptism in the Holy Spirit will bring a greater dimension to _____, but we must make sure that we are located in what God has _____, because this baptism is not for doing that for _____.

31. The Adamic (carnal) nature will still remain with us until _____.

32. Mention some Bible verses regarding the constant struggle between flesh and spirit: _____ _____.

33. <u>What IS the purpose of the baptism in the Holy Spirit:</u>

   a) _____ _____;
   b) _____

_____;
c) _____
   _____;
d) _____
   _____;
e) _____
   _____;
f) _____
   _____;
g) _____
   _____.

34. Who the baptism in the Holy Spirit is for _____.

35. The baptism in the Holy Spirit has the function of equipping us with power for _____.

36. ¿Do we have the right to ask for a special gift? (Confirm your answer with a Bible verse). _____.

37. _____ is the one who distributes the gifts. What is the bible reference? _____.

38. The baptism in the Holy Spirit will give us supernatural power of God for _____ for the purpose of _____ _____ of others.

39. There are those who, having a calling, prefer to preach with "excellence of words or wisdom" and not "_____".

40. The early church lived in the supernatural every day.
☐ True   ☐ False

41. God wrought special _____ by the hands of _____.

42. The evidence of the baptism in the Holy Spirit is _____.

43. These _____ help us pray in a superior dimention to the _____ _____ languages.

44. Being in Christ we do not pray according to _____, but according to _____ _____.

45. There are times we do not know _____ _____ of God. It is then that the Holy Spirit _____ for the saints.

46. When we are baptized "on fire" God lights a _____ inside us so that _____ continuously.

47. The gift of God can be _____ if we stop _____ the fire of God within us, if we stop _____ _____ constantly with the Holy Spirit in _____ Spirit.

48. It is a reality that within Christianity there are different denominations with different points of view but, seeing that the Holy Spirit is poured out on them just like on us, we can say they are our brothers and sisters as well.
☐ True   ☐ False

49. The Lord Jesus Christ said that when the Holy Spirit came down:
a) _____ _____ (John 16:13);
b) _____ _____ (John 14:26).

50. In Acts 1:21-26 the apostles cast lots becau-

se: _____
_____.

51. Everyone that is filled with the Holy Spirit needs to cast lots in the case of an important decision.
☐ True ☐ False

VII. H.

52. Join with a line the following expressions with its corresponding bible verse location:

The gift of the Holy Ghost	Luke 24:49
Receiving the Holy Ghost	Acts 2:33
The Holy Ghost fell	Acts 10:45
The promise of the Father	Mark 1:8
The gift of God	Acts 10:47
The promise of the Holy Ghost	Acts 8:20
Enduement of power from on high	Acts 1:4
Baptized with the Holy Ghost	Acts 11:15

53. Filling of the Holy Spirit and the baptism in the Holy Spirit is exactly the same.
☐ True ☐ False

54. Being filled with the Spirit is more applied _____
_____.

55. In Acts 4:31 can we see that those disciples who prayed had already been baptized with the Holy Spirit, but _____
_____.

56. Not only is it very important to be baptized in the Holy Spirit but even more so to live in that baptism every day until Christ comes.
☐ True ☐ False

VII. I.

57. A person, simply because he is filled with the Spirit, cannot stop making _____ _____ and be responsible for them because God does not _____. He guides us, He orders us, He points us _____ _____ path.

58. The experience of the baptism is only one of several aspects of the Christian life.
☐ True ☐ False

59. What elements of the Christian life can we find in the following verses?
a) 1 Cor. 14:1 _____
_____;
b) 2 Ti. 3:10-11 _____
_____
_____;
c) Gal. 5:22, 23 _____
_____;
d) Eph. 6:10-17 _____
_____.

60. The baptism in the Holy Spirit is the only and greatest gift God has prepared to His children.
☐ True ☐ False

61. He who is baptized in the Spirit enters the _____ where the fight with the enemy is _____. We must therefore arm ourselves with the _____, which is the Word of God.

62. There are times that we can be interceding in the Spirit for someone unknown to us.
☐ True ☐ False

63. Praying in the Spirit is extremely important to those who _____
_____.

VII. J.

64. There are no obstacles to be baptized in the Holy Spirit.
    ☐ True   ☐ False

65. What are the obstacles to receive the baptism in the Holy Spirit?
    a) _____;
    b) _____;
    c) _____;
    d) _____.

66. If the Christian _____ _____ he ceases to be a victor.

67. The baptism in the Spirit is not to sanctify the believer.
    ☐ True   ☐ False

68. Those who constantly ask God for the material for themselves are showing _____ _____ (1 Ti. 6:10).

69. What is the commandment of Jesus in Matt. 6:33? "_____ _____ _____ _____".

70. There is the case of the deceit of the devil to believe that there is _____, because it is imposible that there is no sin.

VIII. The Initial Physical Evidence of the Baptism in the Holy Spirit

1. What book of the Bible is the model for the Lord's church throughout the centuries? _____.

2. We are built upon the foundation of the _____ (Eph. 2:20).

3. In the early church we see _____ that we must follow.

4. Who is saved shows _____ being born again.

5. Who has been baptized in the Holy Spirit manifests _____.

VIII. A.

6. What are the five things the Lord says that would distinguish believers?
   a) _____;
   b) _____;
   c) _____;
   d) _____;
   e) _____.

7. Why when Christ says the five things that would distinguish believers the baptism in the Holy Spirit is not mentioned? _____.

VIII. B.

8. Peter made a difference between the apostles of Christ and those to whom he preached (*see* Acts 2:38-39).
   ☐ True   ☐ False

9. How the Jewish disciples were convinced that the Gentiles received also the baptism in the Holy Spirit? (Acts 10:44-46): _____.

10. The Baptism in the Holy Spirit has no evidence.
    ☐ True   ☐ False

VIII. C.

11. Ignorance about spiritual gifts has _____ in the church of Corinth. It brings _____ to the Church today.

12. Baptism in the Holy Spirit opens the door to the _____.

13. The gift of tongues in the Church requires the _____, otherwise tongues should not be spoken _____ because they do not bring _____ (1 Cor. 14: 4, 5).

VIII. D.

14. Who distributes the gifts of the Spirit? (1 Cor. 12:11)? _____.

15. Can we ask for a particular gift? (1 Cor. 12:31)? _____.

16. The baptism in the Spirit is different than the fruit of the Spirit.
    ☐ True   ☐ False

17. The fruit of the Spirit is the manifestation of _____ in us.

18. Is a requirement to be baptized in the Holy Spirit to manifest the fruit of the Spirit?
    ☐ True   ☐ False

19. To manifest the fruit of the Spirit is equivalent to "walking in the Spirit".
    ☐ True   ☐ False

20. A person could speak in tongues and not walk in the Spirit at the same time.
    ☐ True   ☐ False

VIII. E.

21. If tongues are not interpreted is not good to speak them at any time and place.
    ☐ True   ☐ False

22. According to 1 Corinthians 14:2, the one that speaks in tongues, to whom is speaking to? _____.

23. The kingdom of God is strengthened within us when we _____.

24. It is not only through our intellect that we learn from God and grow. What is another important resource that a Christian can make use? _____.

25. God himself _____ of the Christian when he prays in _____ (Jude 1:20).

VIII. F.

26. When we pray in tongues the Holy Spirit himself intercedes for us through us to the Father about what is convenient for us.
    ☐ True   ☐ False

27. On many occasions we cannot know perfectly _____ on a certain matter and that is where the gift of tongues becomes very important.

VIII. G.

28. How often should we pray in tongues? _____.

VIII. H.

29. When it comes to a meeting, it is better _____ instead of everyone speaking in tongues.

30. To speak in tongues in the service is to speak "on the air," that is, uselessly (if there is no interpretation).
    ☐ True   ☐ False

31. God does not force us to anything, but our spirits are subject to ourselves.
    ☐ True   ☐ False

32. It is a very delicate matter to issue _____ of a manifestation that is not perfectly identified as _____.

IX Sanctification

1. The Bible calls all those who have passed from death to life _____ (Rom. 1:7).

2. It is essential that we are set apart for God and in practice live in _____, because our _____ depends on it, as the Scriptures tell us, "_____" (Heb. 12:14).

3. If there were to be no one who lives in holiness, none will enter into heaven.
   ☐ True ☐ False

IX. A.

4. 1 John 3:4 sin is breaking _____.

5. 1 John 5:17 sin is _____.

6. James 4:17 sin is neglecting _____.

7. God's law has been given to man since creation.
   ☐ True ☐ False

8. Why do we need God's law? (Rom. 3:20). _____.

9. Since a person is born, he is born in sin, and is a sinner by nature.
   ☐ True ☐ False

10. Why a sinner does practice sin? _____.

11. Our attitude against sin is _____, _____, because we are now participants in _____ (2 Pet. 1:4).

12. To say that we are sinners, it is, as the Scriptures say, to make Christ a minister of sin.
    ☐ True ☐ False

13. What does sin produce? Match with a line:

    Lack of spiritual growth   Jer. 5:25
    Obstruction of blessings   Rom. 6:23
    Obstruction of prayers   Dn. 9:7-8
    Hardened the heart   Heb. 12:1
    God's punishment   Ps. 66:18
    Spiritual death   Heb. 3:13
    Confusion   Rom. 6:21
    Dishonor   Heb. 12:6
    Shame   Prov. 14:34

14. To be dead with Him means to be _____.

15. To be resurrected with Him means _____.

16. To be seated in the heavenly places with Him means _____, just as He _____.

IX. B.

17. How can we be sanctified? _____
_____.

18. We are sanctified when we give money to the poor, when we work for free in the church, when we feed the hungry, when we pray, study the Bible and fast.
☐ True ☐ False

19. How can we live in holiness? _____
_____.

20. Believing that our holiness comes from _____ is a deceit of the enemy (Gal. 5:4).

IX. C.

21. What we are in Christ? Match with a line:

    Washed, sanctified
    and justified   Acts 26:18

    Sanctified through the
    offering of His body   Acts 20:32

    Called, sanctified and
    preserved   1 Cor. 1:2

    Called to be saints   1 Cor. 6:11

    Sanctified   Heb. 2:11

    Christ's brethren   Heb 10:14

    We are perfect   Heb. 10:10

    Forgiven and heirs   Jud. 1:1

22. Christ has sanctified us when _____ for us on the cross, and we receive that gift by _____ when we accept Jesus Christ as _____.

23. What does the process of the comprenhension of the doctrine of sanctification consists of? _____
_____
_____.

24. As spiritual children we move on to _____. It means that we have learned to overcome sin through _____.

25. This recognition is achieved when we ____
_____
_____, not only to be saved now, but also to keep us in _____ at every moment, for apart from Him we can do nothing.

26. We are in a constant struggle and the process of this war is until _____
_____.

27. We can read in Jude 1:24 that God is powerful to _____ until our death or until the coming of Christ.

IX. D.

28. We can see in 1Pet. 1:13-15 the progress we need to pass through:
    a) _____;
    b) _____;
    c) _____.

29. For God, who is not clothed with holiness, walks _____ (Rev. 16:15).

IX. E.

30. According to the following Bible verses, what reasons can we find for not sinning?
    ◆ Romans 6:2 because we are _____
    _____;
    ◆ 1 John 3:9 because we are _____
    _____.

31. Galatians 5:24 says: "And they that are Christ's have _____
_____
_____".

33. What is the essential fruit to reach eternal

life? (Rom. 6:22) _____.

34. The devil is lying to us, making us think that we can not _____, ____ but the truth of God is that He gave us victory over sin and by our faith we make _____ dead to sin (Rom. 8:10).

35. We make any thought of temptation _____ _____.

IX. F.

36. Temptation is the same than sin.
☐ True ☐ False

37. How can we escape from temptation? ____ _____ _____ _____.

38. Christ says to us in Matthew 26:41 "_____ _____ _____ _____ _____ _____".

39. Keeping a life of prayer is essential to not enter into temptation.
☐ True ☐ False

40. The Word produces the _____ _____ and keep us in victory against sin.

41. Although a Christian has the new nature, the nature of Christ, he has not discarded the _____. And it is the _____ that manifests passions and desires contrary to _____.

IX. G.

42. When a person becomes a Christian the flesh is eradicated.
☐ True ☐ False

43. Although it is possible that this carnal nature remains cauterized by faith in Christ, that is, insensible or nullified, weakened without strength to act, nevertheless _____ _____ for the moment it can be _____.

44. Our task is to remain in _____ _____, to maintain a life of _____, that is, to _____ _____.

45. What does happen when in a child of God the flesh overcome? _____ _____.

46. We can not deceive ourselves by thinking that we will reach the kingdom of God even if _____ _____.

47. In case of committing a sin we must come immediately to the _____ and _____ _____ to cleanse us from all unrighteousness and to _____ (through faith) _____ in the fear of God.

48. Certainly all the children of God in the whole world and in all times we have had and we have _____, but the difference between those who will have a part in the kingdom of God and those who do not, is their _____ or their _____.

IX. H.

49. Some say that it is impossible to live a life without sin and this is true in some sense if

we consider that there could be moments in the life of a Christian, that due to _____ _____, he falls into some temptation of the flesh or devil's tie.

50. We have everything in God to live minute after minute a life of victory against sin.
    ☐ True ☐ False

51. 1 John 1:8 refers to those who, though ____ _____ _____ _____.

52. There is no such thing as sins that "are hidden from us," for from all sin the Holy Spirit will rebuke us.
    ☐ True ☐ False

53. The words mistake and sin have the same meaning.
    ☐ True ☐ False

54. What is sin is perfectly defined in the Word of God and He does not give us any doubt about what He wants from us.
    ☐ True ☐ False

IX. I.

55. The word in Greek to walk is «stoicheō» and this means _____ _____ _____.

56. For those who walk in the flesh as children of God, and so that they will not be _____ _____, God disciplines or punishes them, so that they may be _____.

57. Due to their _____ _____, a child of God could walk in the flesh. However, not because he is a son _____ has a part with the Lord.

58. God has not disobedient children.
    ☐ True ☐ False

59. Some of the servants of God are unjust, unfaithful, evil and negligent servants.
    ☐ True ☐ False

60. A person totally loses his salvation or his first faith in the moment when the _____ _____ _____.

61. We can use the resource of _____ and _____ as instruments to strengthen our communion with God and our faith in His Word.

62. If a Christian who has the Spirit does not believe the Word expressed in Romans 8:9–11, and does not let the Spirit sanctify him but tries to do it in his own strength, even though the Holy Spirit dwells in him, he will be in the painful and ruinous situation of living in the flesh.
    ☐ True ☐ False

63. We should believe and have full confidence, that simply because the Spirit dwells in us, we have _____ in the Spirit.

64. Why are there those who, having the Spirit of God, sin and are in trouble? _____ _____.

65. Not believing the truth of God in regard to the health of the body leads to _____ _____, however, not believing the truth

of God as to the health of the soul leads to _____.

66. In Romans 8:13 we can see what produces death and what produces eternal life: "_____."

IX. J.

68. In the chapter 4 of Romans we can see that salvation is not by:
   - _____,
   - _____,
   - _____,
   but by _____.

69. The law, instead of producing life in us, produced "sinful passions and fruit for death". Why? _____.

70. This entire chapter 7 of Romans is meant to show us _____.

71. Now we are not under any law (*see* Gal. 6:2) ☐ True   ☐ False

72. The lack of knowledge of this part of the _____ the people of God to _____ (Is. 5:13; Hos. 4:6).

73. Not to live in holiness, means that _____.

IX. K.

74. What is the meaning of striking the body (1 Corinthians 9:25-27)? _____.

75. All the things that the body ask are sinful. ☐ True   ☐ False

76. When it comes to deciding between the comfort of the body and obedience to the Lord we have to be _____.

X   The Church and Its Mission

1. Can a real Christian live in isolation (without a church)? _____.

X. A.

2. Peter established the Church of Jesus Christ.
   ☐ True ☐ False

3. The apostles dedicated their lives to establish insolated Christians instead of groups of believers.
   ☐ True ☐ False

X. B.

4. Who are the members of the Universal Church? _____
   _____
   _____.

5. Among all Christian denominations there may be people washed with the blood of Christ who continue stuck to the true vine that is Jesus Christ.
   ☐ True ☐ False

6. There are religions that help [and promote] this to happen, others are against it.
   ☐ True ☐ False

7. Why is so important to preserve and apply sound doctrine in a church? _____
   _____
   _____
   _____.

X. C.

8. _____ is the body of Christ (Eph. 1:22-23).

9. Those who make up the Church of the Lord are those who remain _____
   _____.

10. To what does the apostle Paul compare the members of the Church in Romans 12: 4-5?
    _____.

11. Based on Ephesians 4:4-6, what are the elements that bring together the Church's members?
    • the same _____,
    • the same _____,
    • the same _____,
    • the same _____,
    • the same _____.

X. D.

12. The main reason why the Church exists on earth is _____
    _____. So that each _____
    _____ knows Jesus and has the opportunity to come to _____
    _____. Then, when a person has been saved, the purpose of the Church is to prepare him so that he (or she) in turn will fulfill the _____ as well.

13. According to 2 Corinthians 5:18 what is the ministry of every one of us? _____ _____.

14. Acts 1:8 says that the purpose of the baptism in the Holy Spirit is _____ _____.

15. When the disciples preached always everybody were converted.
☐ True ☐ False

X. E.

16. What is the meaning of being the fragrant smell of Christ? _____ _____ _____.

17. The church helps each believer to become _____.

18. The concept of worship includes a life of obedience.
☐ True ☐ False

19. Jesus Christ tells us that there are "true worshipers" and that these are those who _____ _____.

20. The adoration that pleases the Lord is born _____, _____ _____, and _____.
Its fruit of _____, but not of _____ only.

21. Worship has to do with _____ (Psalms 130:4).

22. What does sing with intelligence mean? _____ _____.

23. The songs are _____ directed to God that include _____ _____ _____, and these must be in perfect _____ with our faith.

24. Giving _____ _____ to God is also part of our worship of Him (Dt. 16:16; Fil. 4:18).

25. Explain Malachi 3:10: _____ _____ _____.

X. F.

26. What is the foundation of the Church? _____.

27. The Church is the means of God to _____ _____.

28. The purpose of the Church is to edify the spiritual children so that they become _____ and _____ in the doctrine of the Lord and _____ _____.

29. What is the meaning of the word "apostle"? _____ _____.

30. How the word "apostle" is translated by KJV in Philipians 2:25? _____.

31. The _____ are those who are sent by the Lord with a message.

32. To prophesy is to be used by God to _____ _____.

33. Every preacher who is used by God to transmit His message becomes a _____.

34. The prophet is used by God to decipher

mysteries about _____
_____.

35. An evangelist preaches _____ wherever he goes regardless of who the audience is and then goes elsewhere to do the same, leaving the new converts to _____ _____.

36. A pastor is one who _____ _____ of the Lord.

37. The teaching ministry is an integral part of the _____.

38. A teacher has the responsibility to teach by _____ about what he teaches, and to live in _____. (Rom. 2:17-24).

X. G.

39. The book of Acts is _____ and serves as _____ for the Church.

40. Baptism with the Holy Spirit adds a dimension of power to evangelism and brings true growth and supernatural edification to the Church.
☐ True ☐ False

XI The Ministry

1. God has established a spiritual leadership among the people.
   ☐ True ☐ False

2. The triple purpose of this leadership is:
   - _____
     _____ ;
   - _____
     _____ ;
   - _____
     _____ .

XI. A.

3. There is a human leader who directs the Church of Christ in the world.
   ☐ True ☐ False

4. God has established different leadership functions. Who are they _____
   _____ .

5. This position is more of physical service than of spiritual service _____ .

6. The case of Stephen teaches us that a faithful person in a position of physical service can be called by God for spiritual service.
   ☐ True ☐ False

7. The order established by God is that the ministries of _____ and _____ _____ serve the ministers of the gospel, so that they _____ _____ to prepare and serve the church spiritually.

8. Christ Jesus considers the one who serves greater than the one who is served.
   ☐ True ☐ False

XI. B.

9. Although each person is called by God to fulfill the great commission, God has called specific people for the exercise of _____ _____ within the church.

10. There are ministries that have more to do with the physical (and administrative) than with the spiritual and there are ministries that have more to do with the spiritual than with the physical.
    ☐ True ☐ False

11. Mention five names of Bible characters who were called by God: _____
    _____
    _____ .

12. Everyone who was called by Jesus obeyed the calling.
    ☐ True ☐ False

13. What is the meaning of: "the call and the gifts are irrevocable"? _____
    _____
    _____

_____
_____.

XI. C.

14. God is sovereign in the call of His servants and He promotes whoever He wants; however, we know that God will promote the _____ (Ps. 101:6).

15. What is the way to get grace before the Lord? _____
_____.

XI. D.

16. Give two examples of reprobate servants: _____
_____.

17. Paul himself sought at all costs to be _____ and strived every day not to be spoken of as a _____.

18. Paul had no assurance of his salvation.
☐ True ☐ False

XI. E.

19. The call of God requires _____.

20. God strengthens the temperament of the servant according to what God has for him.
☐ True ☐ False

21. The servant must first be willing to go through God's process. This process often involves: _____
_____
_____
_____
_____.

_____
_____
_____.

22. The children of God in general need to remain united to _____, however, a servant of God has a greater responsibility, since they have to be an _____ to the flock.

23. Why did the apostles say, "It is not reason that we should leave the word of God, and serve tables"? _____
_____
_____
_____.

24. The people who are called to a physical ministry must also be _____
_____, but the one who is called to a spiritual ministry occupies most of his time in _____.

25. Why was Paul concerned that his work would not be in vain? (*see* Gal. 3:2-5)? _____
_____
_____
_____.

26. When the gospel is preached, the people are saved, but if they do not persevere in the doctrine of the Lord, the work is lost because those people will not ultimately reach salvation.
☐ True ☐ False

XI. F.

27. According to 1 Pet. 5:4, what is the reward that an approved servant will receive?

_____
_____.

28. How a servant of God must serve to his Master? (*see* 2 Cor. 1:12, Fil. 1:15-17, Heb. 12:28) _____
_____.

29. What we receive here can be compared to what the Lord will grant us in glory.
☐ True ☐ False

30. What is a healthy ambition that God promote? _____
_____
_____.

31. The deceit of the enemy consists in _____
_____
_____ (2 Ti. 4:10).

32. Our reward is totally granted in heaven, not on this earth.
☐ True ☐ False

33. Repeatedly in the Bible we see that it is a pattern that the servants of God in spiritual ministries who work diligently are supported economically by _____
_____ and this support should always be seen as a _____
_____ and never as a _____.
(Mal. 3:10; Fil. 4:17)

XII Divine Healing

1. Christ came to pay the price of both our _____, and our _____ _____.

XII. A.

2. There is a link between spiritual health and health of the soul.
   ☐ True ☐ False

3. In Deuteronomy 28 the Lord tells us about many diseases that are a consequence of _____.

XII. B.

4. The man then dies slowly, but the disease _____.

5. Sickness is an agent of death for all humanity and death is our _____ (1 Cor. 15:26).

6. It is normal for a Christian to die, but it is not God's will that he die because of sickness.
   ☐ True ☐ False

XII. C.

7. The devil did manage to tempt the people of Israel to sin and unleash _____ pronounced by God (Num. 23-25).

8. There is a close relationship between _____ and the disease.

9. According to 1 John 3:8, What did the Son of God come for? _____ _____.

XII. D.

10. Peter points out (although here he refers to suffering) to follow the footsteps of Christ (1 Pet. 2:21), only as regards to suffering or also in His faith? _____ _____.

11. There is a verse in the Bible that says we will do greater works than Jesus, what is this Bible verse? _____.

12. Christ healed all of the sick.
    ☐ True ☐ False

XII. E.

13. Some of those who came to Jesus for physical health returned home sick, because it was not His will to heal them.
    ☐ True ☐ False

14. ¿Which was the answer of Jesus to the man who told him "if thou wilt, thou canst make me clean" (Matt. 8:2) _____.

15. Christ was wounded, he was crushed and punished, he was turned into a wound, so that we _____.

16. Are there cases in the Bible in which someone was not healed? Why? _____

_____.

17. Why in Matthew 17:14-21 Jesus' disciples could not free the child? _____ _____.

18. We need to pray so that the Lord reveals to us His will regarding a specific case of healing because His will regarding divine healing is not clear in the Scriptures.
☐ True   ☐ False

19. Each of the sixteen fundamental doctrines is a matter of faith, and divine healing is not the exception.
☐ True   ☐ False

XII. F.

20. Where can we find in the Bible the definition of faith? _____.

21. "If thou canst _____ _____ that believeth (Mark 9:23).

22. The ministry of Christ was a ministry of salvation of the _____ and healing of the _____, a ministry that continues to _____.

23. God's requirement to receive His promises is always the same: _____ (Matt. 21:22).

24. Who did Paul call "the beloved physician"? (Colossians 4:14) _____.

25. _____ is the evangelist who shows the most miracles of healing in the ministry of Jesus.

26. The sick on the island of Melita came to Luke (as a physician) to receive his help.
☐ True   ☐ False

27. The only time Luke speaks of the healing of the body by human means he did it to discredit the doctors.
☐ True   ☐ False

XII. G.

28. Physician is one of the names of our God.
☐ True   ☐ False

29. Medical science did not bring any benefit to humankind.
☐ True   ☐ False

30. The children of God have their Physician _____.

31. It is our decision to go with the earthly physicians or with the Physicians Jesus of Nazareth.
☐ True   ☐ False

32. Being that the Lord is our Physician, He wants us _____ in His office.

33. With the physicians of this earth it is necessary to take _____ _____; to go with the Celestial Physician, _____ is indispensable.

34. Jesus needs human help to heal us.
☐ True   ☐ False

35. The King, _____ instead of seeking God for healing, sought out the earthly physicians and he _____ (2 Chron. 16:12-13).

XII. H.

36. Paul imitated Christ in everything, also in His faith (1 Cor. 11:1).
☐ True   ☐ False

37. The arguments that say that Paul was sick

perfectly match with the doctrine of divine healing.
☐ True   ☐ False

38. Many Calvinist theologians do not believe in Divine Healing and have permeated their doctrines even among _____.

39. Paul did extraordinary miracles, that is, miracles that stood out to the others performed in the church (Acts 19:11).
☐ True   ☐ False

40. What are the arguments shown by those that believe in the illness of Paul? (include Bible references): _____
_____
_____
_____
_____.

41. The Greek word translated as "infirmity" in Galatians 4:13 also can well be translated as _____.

42. What could be some reasons of physical weakness? _____
_____
_____
_____.

43. Galatia was a Roman province composed of several cities. Amongst these cities were:
_____
_____.

44. Which city was Paul stoned? (Acts 14:1-20) _____.

45. It is therefore very likely that this means that Paul, after being stoned and possibly disfigured, _____ to the Galatians.

46. "And Moses was an _____ _____ years old when he died: his eye was not dim, nor _____ _____" (Deut. 34:7).

47. The two Greek words translated as "large a letter" can well be translated as _____ _____.

48. God sends sickness to those who receive their revelations so that they do not become vain.
☐ True   ☐ False

49. In 2 Cor. 12:10, "therefore" is a linguistic use of transition to give an explanation of what was said _____.

50. Paul's supposed illness is an enemy's weapon to make us _____ about the effectiveness of the blood of Christ and His _____ to heal every _____.

XII. I.

51. Where in the Bible can we find the following words: "But he was wounded for our transgressions, he was bruised for our iniquities: the chastisement of our peace was upon him; and with his stripes we are healed"? _____.

52. Where in the Bible can we find the following words: "Who his own self bare our sins in his own body on the tree, that we, being dead to sins, should live unto righteousness: by whose stripes ye were healed"? _____.

53. The Greek word «sozo» is used interchangeably as _____ and _____ _____ everywhere in the New Testament.

54. When the children of Israel were freed from the bondage of Egypt there was no sick among them.
☐ True ☐ False

55. A person who comes to Him, Christ _____ _____ at the same time.

56. Divine healing is reached through _____ and is for the _____ who live in _____.

57. The devil will flee from us if _____ _____.

58. What do we need to do if there is a sick in the church? (James 5:14-15) _____ _____ _____.

59. What does oil symbolize? _____ _____ _____.

XII. J.

60. The _____ of a disease contradict the word of God because the Bible says that _____.

61. We choose who to believe: the devil who tells us that we are sick or God who tells us that we have already been healed.
☐ True ☐ False

62. It is about believing His Word about our new life in Christ and the aspect of the _____ of the body cannot be the _____, in fact our body is _____, it is the body of Christ.

XII. K.

63. Illness does not bring glory to God.
☐ True ☐ False

64. We cannot do with the body of Christ (which is our body) what we want, but instead we must submit it to the Lord, bring it _____ _____ living sacrifice.

65. Christ claims His body, that we _____ _____ and that we do not _____ _____ for the sake of serving Him.

66. The food we eat is _____ to a person's health.

67. Why is praying for our meals important? _____ _____ _____ _____.

68. Mention some verses of the Bible where God promises to bless our meals _____ _____ _____.

69. In addition to being careful with food we eat and praying for our meals, what can we do to take care of our bodies? _____ _____ _____.

XII. L.

70. What sin is for _____, disease is for _____, so we must _____ _____ both evils.

71. Sickness cannot give glory to God, as sin will never bring glory to God.
☐ True ☐ False

72. Christ came to destroy the _____ _____ and both _____ and _____ _____ are Satan's work.

73. Of those who put themselves in the hands of human physicians, some are cured by them, others get worse and others (as in the case of Asa) even die.
☐ True   ☐ False

74. When the church of the Lord returns to the original doctrine of Divine Healing, God will use it for the healing of many and provoke _____ _____ _____.

XIII Blessed Hope

1. As in the case of the Galatians, Paul warns the Corinthians that it is indispensable to remain in the pure doctrine of the gospel in order to _____.

XIII. A.

2. What does the hope that Peter spoke consist of? (1 Pet. 1:3; Rom. 14:9)? _____
_____
_____.

3. The foundation of our resurrection is that _____
_____.

XIII. B.

4. Draw a line to connect the verse with its scripture reference:

"I will not leave you comfortless: I will come to you"   Rev. 22:7

"And if I go and prepare a place for you, I will come again, and receive you unto myself; that where I am, there ye may be also"   John 14:18

"Behold, I come quickly: blessed is he that keepeth the sayings of the prophecy of this book"   John 14:3

"And, behold, I come quickly; and my reward is with me, to give every man according as his work shall be"   Rev. 3:11

"Behold, I come quickly: hold that fast which thou hast, that no man take thy crown"   Rev. 22:12

5. Those of us who have been born again and are prepared for his coming with garments of holiness, will be _____.

6. Paul tells us that those who died in Christ will experience the _____ _____, then those who are alive will be _____ _____ _____ (1 Thes. 4:16-17).

7. Who died in Christ will _____ _____ and will live again, but in a _____ body.

XIII. C.

8. How can we describe the word "sudden"? _____
_____.

9. The rapture will not be instantaneous.
☐ True   ☐ False

10. What is the meaning of the word "imminent"? _____
_____
_____.

11. In Matthew 25 the Lord urges His people to be always _____ _____.

12. The Lord tells us that His coming will be at an _____, that He will come as a _____. (1 Thes. 5:2).

13. What is the meaning of "watch!"? _____ _____ _____.

14. There are some who have argued that it is not yet imminent because the Lord made it a requirement upon His return that the gospel be preached in all the world.
☐ True ☐ False

15. The imminence of the coming is a teaching of _____.

16. The disciples were waiting for the coming of the Lord.
☐ True ☐ False

17. When was the prophecy of the preaching of the gospel throughout the world fulfilled? _____ _____ _____.

18. If we believe that Christ cannot come yet, because there are no nations or ethnic groups to which the Gospel has not been preached, based on a _____, we would have to demolish dozens of others who claim that the Lord's coming (the rapture) is _____ and the apostles were _____.

XIII. D.

19. Our glorified body will have characteristics similar to the _____ _____ (1 John 3:2).

20. Draw a line to connect the characteristic of our glorified body with its scripture reference:
    It can passes through walls   Matt. 26:29
    It can have scars   Dn. 12:3
    It can be touched   1 Cor. 15:43
    Able to disappear   Luke 20:36
    Powerful   John 20:20
    Asexual   John 20:17
    A spiritual body   Luke 24:31
    Incorruptible   John 21:12
    Shinning   Matt. 22:30
    It can not die   1 Cor. 15:42
    Different appearance   John 20:26
    Able to eat and drink   1 Cor. 15:44

XIII. E.

21. How can we be prepared to the Lord's comming? _____ _____.

22. 1 Thessalonians 5:4 says: "But ye, _____ _____ _____ _____."

23. What is the sign to know that we are prepared to the rapture? _____ _____.

24. Those who are of the world practice sin (Rom. 1:32), and even if they do not _____ directly, they engage in _____ (Matt. 24:38, Luke 21:34), and in matters related to _____ and _____ in marriage (Matt. 24:38), and they are idle to _____ the Lord (Matt. 25:24–30).

25. For the children of God who now live in _____ He has patience,

and He gives them _____, since they are His _____, and He does not want them to _____ (2 Pet. 3:9).

XIII. F.

26. The second comming of Christ and the rapture are the same.
    ☐ True ☐ False

27. Place the following events in order (from first to last):
    ____ The battle of Armageddon
    ____ The great tribulation
    ____ The rapture of the church
    ____ Millennium
    ____ Tribulation period
    ____ Visible coming of Christ

28. Draw a line to connect the event with its scripture reference:

    The battle of Armageddon   1 Thes. 4:16-17
    The great tribulation   Rev. 11:3
    The rapture of the Church   Matt. 24:21
    Millennium   Rev. 16:16; 19:19
    Tribulation   Rev. 19:11-21
    Visible coming of Christ   Rev. 20:6

29. Meanwhile, in these period of tribulation and the great tribulation, in total seven years, _____ will be at the _____ _____ in _____.

XIII. G.

30. God says there will be no more _____ for the _____ but this will be for the _____ _____ (2 Thes. 1:6-9).

31. Mention two more bible verses as proof that the Church will not pass the great tribulation period: _____.

32. What is the belief that the Church will pass the great tribulation called? _____.

33. In 2 Thessalonians 2:1-12 we can read something called "the day of the Christ", what is this about? _____.

34. Draw a line to connect the characteristics of the day of the Lord with its scripture reference:

    Day of destruction   Ez. 30:3
    It will come as a thief   1 Thes. 5:2-4
    Day of punishment for the nations   Is. 13:9
    Day of wrath and fierce anger   Joel 1:15

35. What is holding the antichrist from being revealed? _____.

XIII. H.

36. Why does the Church work while waiting for the Lord's coming? _____.

XIV. The Millennial Kingdom of Christ

1. The battle that will be the culmination of the time of the antichrist is calleed _____ _____.

2. The beast and the false prophet will be imprisoned and _____ _____ (Rev. 19:20).

3. What is the role of the false prophet? _____ _____ _____.

4. What will happen with Satan after the battle of Armageddon? _____ _____.

XIV. A.

5. Who will reign with Christ in the millennium? _____ _____ _____.

XIV. B.

6. Write down the characteristics of Christ reign:
   a) _____ _____;
   b) _____ _____;
   c) _____ _____;
   d) _____ _____;
   e) _____ _____;
   f) _____ _____;
   g) _____ _____;
   h) _____ _____;
   i) _____ _____;
   j) _____ _____;
   k) _____ _____;
   l) _____ _____;
   m) _____ _____;
   n) _____ _____.

7. All God's children will have part with Christ in the millennium.
   ☐ True   ☐ False

XV The Final Judgment

1. The Final Judgment is called the judgment of the _____.

XV. A.

2. After the millennium, Satan will be released for an indeterminate period of time.
   ☐ True   ☐ False

3. How will the Lord defeat His enemies in the battle of Gog and Magog? _____
   _____
   _____.

4. When all determined things on earth are concluded, the judgment of the _____
   _____ begin.

XV. B.

5. Who will be in this judgment? _____
   _____
   _____
   _____.

6. There are three groups of people that we know for sure are not going to suffer the second death, what are they? _____
   _____
   _____
   _____
   _____.

_____
_____.

XV. C.

7. We now have the knowledge that the Lord will be the judge of the living and the dead, what does this knowledge warn us about?
   _____
   _____
   _____.

8. What could be compared to the privilege of entering eternal life? _____.

9. In Revelations 21:8 we can read another list of those who will not enter in the kingdom of God: _____
   _____
   _____
   _____.

XV. D.

10. With God's children, His judgment in this life is for _____.

11. God justifies the sinner by the perfect sacrifice of Christ, and that he overlooks the sins of the one who is ignorant of the gospel at the moment he comes to the Lord with repentance and faith.
    ☐ True   ☐ False

12. Although the Lord forgives our sins after we are converted to Christ, the repercussions of them will come.
☐ True ☐ False

13. Then the _____ of each one will be _____ and the book of _____ will be opened.

14. God's children are left with the _____ that God has according _____ _____ (1 Cor. 3:8).

15. All our work will be tested according to _____ (1 Cor. 4:5).

XV. E.

16. 1 Corinthians 3:13 says: _____
_____
_____
_____
_____
_____
_____.

XV. F.

17. Having said all of the above, we must be careful of _____, for of every _____ we will have to give an account (Matt. 12:36), of our _____ (1 Cor. 3:13) and of the _____ of our hearts about anything (1 Cor. 4:5), because even though it now seems that _____, one day God will bring all things to judgment and _____ will be manifest.

XVI. A New Heaven and A New Earth

1. After the judgment of the Great White Throne, he Lord will bring us to the _____ _____.

2. 2 Peter 3:13 tells us about certain things that will be new, what are they? _____.

3. The New Jerusalem will come down from the new heaven.
   ☐ True ☐ False

XVI. A.

4. Who is the architect and builder of the New Jerusalem? _____.

5. Its street is of _____, it is sea of _____, its gates are _____ and the names of the _____ upon them; and on its twelve foundations the _____ _____, engraved.

6. In this city there is no night.
   ☐ True ☐ False

7. Within the city there is a _____ of water of life, which shines like _____ and comes out of the _____ _____.

XVI. B.

8. Paul says: "Having therefore these _____ _____, dearly beloved, let us cleanse ourselves from all _____ _____ and _____, perfecting _____ in the fear of God" (2 Cor. 7:1).

9. All of us who are _____ of the New Jerusalem live as _____ in this world.

Final Note

1. What is the reason for failure in the Christian life? _____.

2. But as of today, the kingdom of heaven is _____ by brave men and women, who occupy _____ in the _____ of God and in _____ that they produce.

How to be HEALED by God even if doctors say it's IMPOSSIBLE

It doesn't matter what your symptoms or your medical conditions are right now, whether it be cancer, diabetes, high blood pressure, or any other sickness which has been said there is no cure for, if you are willing to learn and follow the Gospel's truths you will be healed. God gave us a wide range of blessings which include not only the opportunity to be saved but to be physically healthy as well. Andrew Murray explains all this in his book, *Divine healing*. A book that has sold thousands of copies since it was published.

We all have gotten sick at some point in our lives. Even Christians have gotten sick and some have died because of it. But, why would this happen if God has said we all have been healed already? Can a Christian go to the doctor's or should he/she wait for God's will to be done? How can we ask God in a prayer for healing and be heard? How long does it take God to answer prayers? Does God punish sinners by giving them a disease? In this book, you can find the answers to these and many other questions you may have about this topic.

In this book you will learn:

1. Bible verses in which you can base your prayer in order to be healed.
2. How to pray to be heard by God and get the answer to your prayer.
3. Why maintaining a constant communion with God is indispensable.
4. Why it is important to forgive and live a Holy life.
5. When is it correct to go to the doctors.
6. Where to get faith to be healed.
7. How many times should one pray in order to be healed.

Andrew Murray, the author of this book, was also sick for a certain period of his life. For more than 2 years he was not able to speak. As soon as he placed his trust in the Divine Doctor, he was not only rewarded by divine healing but with an amazing understanding of this topic about which he talks in his book.

More about Andrew Murray:

- Son of Scottish parents but born and raised in South Africa (1828-1917).
- He obtained his theological education in the Netherlands.
- He went back to South Africa as Pastor and missionary.
- He's considered the most influential Christian writer during the XIX century and one of the most influential writers of all time.
- He wrote more than 240 books and tracks in English and Dutch.
- His books exceed the two million copies sold.

The time for you to be healed has come. Thousands of people have been healed by understanding God's will and the main steps that need to be followed to obtain divine healing. God is giving us the opportunity so that we don't doubt his plans and be able to rejoice in perfect health. Click on the "Buy now" button for you to have the book and be blessed with it.

www.ingramcontent.com/pod-product-compliance
Lightning Source LLC
Chambersburg PA
CBHW081757100526
44592CB00015B/2464